Words that Mattered in the Moment

poetry by

Nicholas Skaldetvind

Clare Songbirds Publishing House Poetry Series
ISBN 978-1-947653-98-6
Clare Songbirds Publishing House
Words that Mattered in the Moment© 2021 Nicholas Skaldetvind

All Rights Reserved. Permission to reprint individual poems must be obtained from the author who owns the copyright.

Cover illustrations © Wen Tang, 2021
Author Photo © Danielle Rubi, 2021

Printed in the United States of America
FIRST EDITION

Clare Songbirds Publishing House was established to provide a print forum for the creation of limited edition, fine art from poets and writers, both established and emerging. We strive to reignite and continue a tradition of quality, accessible literary arts to the national and international community of writers, and readers. Chapbook manuscripts are carefully chosen for their ability to propel the expansion of art and ideas in literary form. We provide an accessible way to promote the art of words in order to resonate with, and impact, readers not yet familiar with the siren song of poets and writers. Clare Songbirds Publishing House espouses a singular cultural development where poetry creates community and becomes commonplace in public places.

140 Cottage Street
Auburn, New York 13021
www.claresongbirdspub.com

Contents

Things to Do in Copenhagen (Denmark	7
Acting Apart	10
Spectral	11
Abundance	13
A Chance	14
The Woods	16
Thayer Glimpse Revisited	17
Commenting	18
Mirroring Custom	20
Lunar Majesty	22
Quick Haiku	23
Sleepwalking	24
Did You See Me Bicycling by the Lakes?	26
Together with Someone Else	27
Morning in Boulder	29
Francis and Ignatius Would Move Through the Imperfect Medium of Skaldetvind in an Authentic New York School Poem	30
The Coast	31
Locating	32
Distances	33
Termoli Chant	34
Autumn's Equinox	35
Monologue	36
Theo-logy	37
Alis Volat Propriis	38
Flying Stand-by	40
I Went to D.H. Lawrence's Ranch	41
San Luis Obispo	42
Quaresima	44
Westward Reflection	46
Tuesday Morning Trying on Death	48
Broad Creek Run	49
Currently	50
Sonnet 70, Massachusetts	52
Renga	53
Skaneateles Post Office	54
END	55

Some of the poems have appeared previously in *Wisdom Body Collective* and *Two Thirds North*, to whom the poet and publisher offer their thanks.

In one breath the poet would like to salute affections old and true and he would also like to admit that sometimes the best word in the moment is no word.

Things to Do in Copenhagen (Denmark)

Assume everyone you meet wants to sleep with you,
                 but don't let on
because that's bad form
        especially when
you know that size matters.
You have everything you could possibly dream of
        when
you wake up, stretching your tired flesh
in a new morning's low lying bed,
contriving the necessary resources of last night's lust to continue & at a
certain point begin to
wonder how it all might fall together, so you roll over in eyeless rage
                there are so many factors engaging your attention!
Bicycle on &
everyone is turned on in their certain way
& making it no secret
& when you thought
"she actually loves me"
the rain began to come down
from spherical pre-dominances
beckoning groaning travel (or travail if you prefer)
"let's make this work"
                exhausting life,
so effortlessly universal are the perils of just aimlessly sitting
          with the network
you travel with
                          &
by the thousands of crowns,
enkindle all the sparks of your nature
gone, lit up
in spliff after spliff after spliff
afterwards boring feelings arise
compelling you
        to drink more,
& then   dress
in a reactionary,
minimalistic black,
so you're cool now
& so you see a new expensive film where no one can see you &
contemplate the meaning but not for long when you realize you're out
of money &
smoking borrowed cigarettes, decide to read an underwhelming, gut

wrenching old man's take on life:
THE LITTLE MERMAID or
FEAR AND TREMBLING – overcome by the same
stagnant change,
                        flashback
Play chess on Staden,
                                      study something,
start to sound clever, scratch your balls in public in the great serenade of
things
you experience dirty paranoid thoughts desirous of summer storms
flooding
canal swells following a face you thought you recognized show tender
mercy
towards something or someone old, like how a monument weeps in
May's frozen tears
melting into June (also like how your heart mattered in that moment)
"sometimes I feel like Jagtvej could go on forever"
"where's the ashtray?"
"who's that at the door?"
it's Heaven's benedictions knocking through
sacred radiances of the sun
glinting in clinking bicycles above harbor boats
gliding over quiet, cloudy waters, winds
of persecuting Chlamydia sky
howl in a baby's cry as Holy water from Heavenly eye
less rage,
                        catch it and you're dead, man
caught in a best friend's toothy smile,
another monument of yours as you might like to consider it poetic to
sing guttural rhymes in certain clamorous catch phrases
whiling away small talk Time
    & raising questions about the weather –
                slowly   it   goes,
you go your gait, apace
your happy lifestyle advances
like some kind of cool unperturbed buoy on tour in a Baltic tempest &
understanding this weirdly in mind & that in fact
            you move from the womb to the tomb alone
                you might speak about it
enough and enough
and in between?   work, curse,
fuck
through your soul's inadequacy of come-ons & putdowns
love the state, get paid, hate on The States,

go on a thousand dates in gardens,
celebrate the birth of friends' comforting well-informed ignorance
melancholically, mechanically, dutifully
say the same thing back and forth through the pendulous air
treasuring secretly the part of you that individually
changes,
                        like tricking yourself to be concerned with respectable
things, wanting & getting your way so
your parents, & don't stop there
your friends' parents regard you in the highly coveted
pragmatic light, unspoken-ly   &
privately yearn for more sun, complain
but just a little,   &
love that girl forever,
love Denmark forever,
make hyggelige memories forever,
Go away   & soon forget.

Acting Apart

Breathing in
makes him more cautious

You might say that he had an air of keeping himself disengaged
from the mere words he let drop

His verbs were catapults for his adverbs and datives
visible syllables springing up like well-tended roses.
For almost the first time he had the feeling he was acting a part

She longed to be a nourishing bosom for the infant Earth,
but was too narrow and weary

He knew she wondered why she had coaxed the writhing vines of her
devotion onto
such a wind-shaken, pompous genius of the Genus Populus
and because of this
she did not leave him

**

We should not give so much practical meaning to our lively endeavors
they don't want to be bothered
they do not bother

**

Still
An ecstasy of eternal seconds
A pulse harder than gravity

**

I felt like talking to those lovers under the sea
so I picked up a shell nearby
held it to my ear

What I heard was suspended
black velvet
silence.

Spectral

To Johanna Norrbin

Abashed and smiling
the elements of disbelief are strongest in the morning, and
night is a room darkened for lovers

We lie in faces vacant of intent,
our round-eyes subdued
by each other
a pellucid and unwavering sight as I feel yours on mine

Breathing the sprinkled stars alive in concentric dilations,
I prop myself up by elbows in one
tensible spectrum of love and fear
a strange angle against the gravity
of your shy thighs
pulling me in half blind so that I inevitably
lose myself up to my hips
in yours

The promise of pleasure costs more
than the repository might hold

What have I made you into?

Tawdry veined, you hold me
growing in your hand I push apart
two dimpled knees opening and closing them
like two startled trout
half cold, half full of light
lost in between and within strained, and
warmer than I ever imagined

Words exploding of their own volition, we begin to outdo one another.

Your eyes reveal two dawns colored by the bed
Yes I said Yes I will and you as you said,
Pale as seashells veils of clarity slowly blink
as if eternity rested there on your eyelids
I said Yes my heart is going like mad in an intermittent state
half musing, half watching one another
there are two planes of consciousness open

I am half rapt, half aware of what is passing under my vision
as the opening in the morning wall dimly glows
blinding the closed space of our slumbering fathoms
boring in between motes of floating dust

Risking joy in the new awakening,
I feel the pressing need to adjust the
mechanisms of perception pressing in
a far away stare
with your finger entwined in mine within the socket of your waist
so we know we are spinning by the warp of the world

We breathe tryst of spontaneity,
a palpable emanation of light in darkness

Complications arise
the world comes in quick, you'll go your way and I mine
and we are lost to one another in the wake of morning.

Abundance

life in abundance
thronging lights of bliss
a reticent clock on the window
syllabic oneness.
Shorter hours long—
ing days noticing your
voice next to mine, soft
pestilence of spit
orienting one choice
perception open
appearing to us
as things already
are infinitely
clear in abundance.

A Chance

To Simone Brandt Thygesen

I am lying in the farmer's field alone
under the dark promise of night
surging across the ageing
star sprinkled sky
stabbing a blue light dilating
my eyes in the art
of moon-gazing, wet
and tilted and half gone,
where there are no mirrors, remembering us

Over my head the barren poplars
gleam on the field's perimeter
looking at them is like looking down
an endless hall of mirrors, all branches,
because now alight in waning moonlight
the poplars look like crowns of brown tassel
flailing, bristling audibly almost
as if whispering words that mattered in the moment
in soft echoes of yore through your
flute of pallid moonlit lips veiled
by the exact clarity of the poplar brown
of your hair and I paused to chance a reticent glance, at
you, not knowing for how long I'd rest in the moment

I mused we were individual stars
in one constellation falling on the edge of sleep
my cheek against yours against our pulse
crossing our one soul in one beat across the pillow's
upturned cheek ipso facto producing a quiver
in space, in blood
so that our secret longings forced themselves forth
unperturbed by the space constraints of bedroom Time
"a baby together"
when we promised to learn the skills for gathering food,
almost a renaissance of our own on the coast

Seldom bothered we each were to do so
but if you ever wanted to see my perspective, you would see I am here now
aging and fulfilling other obligations under some neutral force
where my breath softly echoes consoling whispers
consciously present or not to myself that you entered my life by chance

the inexactness of quoting a fact in the same way the starlit poplar surf
reaches across the cheek of the beach into a distant memory where
waves now
become words in a farmer's field alone.

A mirror makes two, and that is a blessing

If you saw what I see you'd see self-delusion in me

Ghoul faced beneath the flailing branches I confess this
to the tenebrous boughs murmuring the gossip of the grasses,
to the stellar light's slumber of glinting surf,
to you
slipping away and the whole
spring's flowering darkness
that our immediacy calculated against us

Raising tearful eyes, I can see we each have done the things we desired,
sometimes together, other times on our own,
an algebra of sad lyricism which we might still be equating
but regardless of our inconsistent idealism,
our temperate chance of unity was destined to endure as an unsolved
loneliness
shaped in passing and coming in from all sides

The silent crop of stars grows
and I've gone to sleep somewhere between
Earth and space.

The Woods

To Zoe Moncheur

Migrating beyond the void of those sad certainties
winters and summers
falling upon us
your respiration stirring
small leaves alive sacrificed
by the scythe of sullen death
in my mind preceding the lascivious dream
of spring in a forest
and the flowers right before
the bird's eye view
and the stem of the sun's narrow blue eye
fixed upon bough in a squall of leaves
shrilling the upright bodies of castrated winter trees
caught by the look of love bursting
at us being born in a thrusting sunder,
an awakening fire through the trees

A roar of memory
tombstone still
for a passing of time
never up to you nor I
until it is time for life
in the world's turning woods
when we begin to stir

We stir, are stirring
we are still, still stirring
underneath
remembering lips once
touching, wondering,
whether or not
scars kissing scabs
reveal pain

> When we kiss it is like gilded butterflies
> Being born everywhere
> Inside our eyelids

The flower is spring's dream
and if you bite my cheek with illusions of a forest flower
I might forget while spring remembers that
eating the sun is a flower's dream.

Thayer Glimpse Revisited

To Eva Mae

I brought you by the hand under the moonlike lamplight
of Thayer Park, which is the park of the world, where we traipsed
feeling lit-up seeing light bulbs in late autumn daylight as a real luxury

Astray you walked through the day's streaming luminosity
between laughing pillows gliding by like years, swinging limbs, trespassing
your hand against my arm under cold serried pines writhing in space
orchestrating sad seasonal music. Beyond the colorful needles I followed
your forefinger far out tracing the green park
bench, where we sat side-by-side above the ordinary blue lake enjoying our
divertissement

You popped sunflower seeds in my mouth one at a time as if each were a
joke and got up.
I saw that the circular itinerary of the park, which is the park of the world,
would bring you back to me goose-like in sight of the sparkling bench, the
quality of which you said came
from my green eyes—you lovely mammal— that got me started circling
after a metaphor for life

I crossed my legs at you. You touched my nose as if some lost memory of
youth were coming
into view. We were near-lovers as a nearby rodent chased another one

Holding a town meeting, the geese squawk the news of the world in unison
as if trying to recall something forgotten. At once I imagine they landed on
the world's lake of a thousand white horses without knowing what would
come next

I looked up at your big squirrel eyes alive
with a gust of wind I guessed
the itinerary of the world's lives
brought you here to aimlessly take a glimpse at mine
by the hand under the moonlike lamplight of Thayer Park, which is the park
of the world.

Commenting

The sublime simplicity of reality.

Jagged peaks remain silent
before the inexperience of life and
the ignorance of vice
while I watch a certain slant of sunlight appear behind
their kin casting long sharp living shadows of lilac daylight
across the valley
in no word of comment

On some peak's acme I am holding my breath
in homage to the pulsing heart beats
of the whole darkened valley
before the rising dawn
I hear the mountain prophets
preach to all walks of life, to all saviors of ideals, to all conceivable backgrounds
of drawing water from one river, one tarn, under one tree, over one rock,
in no word of comment

To the people who share the same thought
of the same flowing river,
an eddy of hope
waits for you
dear, mediocre man you
full of praise for things you do not know
in wholehearted gratitude
in no word of comment

Setting out on one path with two ends,
never the both seen
in a single frame of angry winds
sweeping docile eyes at established and proven worries
while I follow the ridgeline down a landscape
of heat, singing my feet where
the primeval dawn falls
on summer rock under
the passivity of Earth aglow.
No single place better
than the one I left
behind pressing forward
with animated pulses crossing

in no word of comment

All paths ark towards the dawn
bodies of light
creeping in yawns
together for one common fantasized
bed of a celestial brightness,
an ethereal beauty,
my solitude flows onward with the river
in no word of comment

How did I get here?
I ask myself exploring
the idea of freedom
an eclipse, an ellipse of infinite emptiness
this privileged moment
of rapture entwining this ribbon
of territory from where I do not stray
in no word of comment

I follow myself down
in a mix-up of molecules, all the while
harkening these peaks' message
in no word of comment

(The perfect word as I tell it to you, poor sweet categorizers: I am
ephemeral and nothing matters except harmony in everything.)

Mirroring Custom

When I thought I knew everything
I cut out towards the hills beyond
letting the knapsack of custom
slide off my back with each step
across the breadth of the continent

All my nerves quivered
as if they were a votive bouquet,
an offering to the Earth's vibrating plane
for every flesh and bone tabernacle
embedded in the dirt

My moods created judgment
about how it must feel
to cross great distances
it is almost to understand how a storm feels
to a tree sucking in the sky
with leaves fluttering drily and bitten
saffron by the sun and clinging
as if loathe to let go
uprooted and leaving
a bough now
tree-wise in enduing bare ridges

Or hearing the music of the wind
ruffling the river's swift and fleeting
immense intensity
within the Earth's rolling Cathedral,
glinting light on the surface

These sweeping maneuvers leave seekers and thieves alike unsure
if temptation's supplication
is an earnest hope of wanting to learn
everything in this trivial world
which seems like nothing
like the water's message of paralytic rills in rippled river lines
is a suggestion of light feet everything teeming
ephemeral and primordial at once,
seeming like nothing

And I look up to the mountains
with their faces unchanged
their weightless proposals
and landscape of mind are immeasurable
in their scope
and are in fact mine too

The exultant and free cathedrals
are found where you only have
the mechanism of your own perception
to calculate
intentions imaginative,
realizations relentless
with solely your shadow behind you as reminiscent
of a past life that bore
close proximity of all things enduring
as soon as you're willing to get
somewhere
sometime.

Lunar Majesty

The two luminaries confronted each other across the land.
I am the slow-moving moon's prince, or squire, or at least here
seated supine under a little oak
making funny faces
in the magnificent clear-edged lunar-blur
opening up to fragments alive as if I'd been
here before unattached to any particular history
asking myself how it might be so
that permanence and ephemerality coexist.
Am I here for reasons different than why I am here now?
Certainly reasons more ancient, more serious, more simple

The moon
Her lunar eyes raying astral influences
so that the insects may cease
in homage to the waxing mirth
moondrowning light.
Anon I roll over,
cross my legs slack-faced and relaxed absolve all I can
nodding breathlessly
in homage to Her majesty.

Quick Haiku

Pressing my nose in
sands smelling the shadow of
ancient volcano.

Sleepwalking

To Susan

I stagger thru the hard contours of her sleeping.
The tremendous grades of separated sound
incised among staggering angles
I pull myself up against her fits of gravitating
ridges of night layered ego-dream
giving up to cosmic carnal senses

From my dream's corner in a blind world of fierce abstraction
there stretches a flattering falsehood of sleep, pocketed
in dark immobile silence into shrieks waking in juxtaposes and
in so doing, breaking it
when she asks,
do you remember
what you do
in my dreams?
a fleeting afterthought now
as I lurk through the landscape unseen
she lives in with her mind undone
slowly unfolding as a bud
does underwater

Awake or not I say,
I'll try to remember
I came to view the elements of night that we both share
seeing her now shivering, now exhaling
breaths to sweep the fallen blossoms
and I tell myself that's all anyone can do

Eyes a flame of excitement
a fire of blood
changes in a blink of her eye, in me
to sluggish ice
a cry of anger
dies away to a gurgling
in her throat

Minute muted darkness
veiling the mind's indifferent voluminous monologue
where there emerges a telepathic faculty
though we think differently at night, the thought still matters in the moment

she once told me
crossing over and languidly relapsing
into a cross-legged lotus saying,
remember this image
before closing your eyes

How can I say
my mind is a pillow
and a fleeting dream is cool
alive with an animal alertness
we still stumble into each other
towards dawn's thin daylight
defiantly we each admit
beyond words
that in sleep we dream the same dream.

Did You See Me Bicycling By The Lakes?

I was thinking of you
drinking a Fynsk Forår in heat
it was the brown bottle sweating, pressing into your long expressive
fingers slowly tanning, mostly burning in the oppressing heat, but it was
your face

I saw on a square
H&M ad, no it was Ragnhild's—
but I was thinking of you

as I waited in my lane for the light to change
before the raised harbor bridge where the boats in their shimmering distance
mysteriously disappear below,
I was thinking of you in twitching neon at dusk
the bridge lowered, and
as the sky grew feeble
the sun sank in my eyes, and
I was thinking of you, and
right now.

Together with Someone Else

To Daphne Abildskov

All the ways to say I'm sorry never mean much. For instance you walk in and collapse behind the descending dusk's door in the blue bedroom's ego-dream creating illusions of love living in the corner and I am overcome by the effortless anesthetic effect of a transient habit watching you anxiously get up with downcast eyes traversing the lopsided bedroom floor of my life

One bedroom is all I'll ever have in eternity

There is a neurotic coherence we take on in bedroom words as the shared series of strokes
that complete the form before the transitory door closes on all the forgotten faces.
Enthralled by the space we share, we go about preparing ecstatic excuses back and forth until you face me saying, It's a matter of formlessness you exhibit when we're apart
Well what do you expect? Something defined and symmetrical?

Everything behaves with a suspicious air obeying a few impulses.
The prismatic angst of cacti succulents hang by chains
swaying from the ceiling, groping the wall against your fingers (with love)
pulling me toward the floor
you reach for the stars
heralding the moment bound to follow, grabbing instead
the far side of the infinite, which is a very existential place

We collapse like we've done so many times together before, other times with someone
else you hide the velvet thought from me between your crossed legs
offering a whole series of bedrooms which you've crossed
shifting and adapting and after so much time acting apart, I know by
now it is your shapely warm
center where I want to be feeling rather than seeing your smile

From west coast to east coast
to nowhere
penitent and hurt by real love
and false love too

All those summers, all those lovers back and forth across the bedroom

floor and everything still continues to be possible together.
The insolent indifference of the summer fan is a faithful guardian
of far distant days droning its "yeahs" amid our airless uncertainties as
if we were not there
to its own silver steel vader hum steady and stable and
even more so in this moment, hand in hand in the same room.

Morning in Boulder

To Jen Clausen & Jim Ellis

"I love how straight those colorful flowers are - you know how our
tulips at home usually droop over at the top?"
***
Cursing myself for getting hung up on big terms like eschatology,
at first I didn't know if they were tulips along the median
wondering what to do with ourselves
on downtown Boulder's brick promenade
the morning sun on our skin, a dead leaf scraping around phos-
phorescent flowers I knew we weren't in Lisbon or Paris or Co-
penhagen with their fuming cars and pedestrians we were in thin
rocky mountain country air—time's dizzying stars filling my
lungs
(memory and dream mixing)
the long ghosts who passed before me for another chance at light
Cassady full of promise, jumping naked from a second-story bathroom
window into a cold Larimer Alley where he waited all afternoon titter-
ing over his pecker tracks for Mary—Time had no home in him—
Kerouac traipsing the void in beat huaraches somewhere between
Cheyenne and Denver, in hopes of catching that last thing once
and for all - a body lit with love under the sun
rushing along the downtown redbrick of his Chinese mystery—
a school here named after him,
the same school where Jen planned to study botany.
Jen, whose big secret eyes, almost loving me, are
hidden in the passenger seat "These are my ways.
It hurts too much loving you."
We drove on and on, in pain
a forgotten star burned over the eastern plains
in the red immersion of another day,
I ask if this feeling of infinity is too close?
My eyes hurt, and I'm out of money.
(memory and dream mixing)
Starved for companionship in a premonition of movement,
Lawrence's arid pines waver with the memory
of Jen behind the wheel (memory and dream
mixing)
in the botanical gardens of Kings
"Which way should we go?"
"Let's keep going straight."

Francis and Ignatius Would Move Through the Imperfect Medium of Skaldetvind in an Authentic New York School Poem

      Indefinable, ample, rhythmic frame
      now here,
most unworthy though I am standing perfectly still before an infallible
statuary saint of untiring apostolic zeal, barefoot, at 19:13 (that's p.m.)
in 24-hour Colorado Heaven.
   The year is unaccountable. It's 2021. The air is inky and viral.
On the way to pray—
er, I drink in some fierce ponderosa pine needle vapor and ascend. The
retreating grounds look clean as o negative blood in bare feet, or as divine
illuminations together with all other spiritual relish. Above the parapet
of Heaven I wonder what fantasies of the Eucharist will this all lead to?
I smile at the spectacle and expel a touch of gas.
   Who in California would have dreamt that I'd be here?
Not good old Cody Moriarty, or all of David Krowitz's goons put together,
or Syd CalFresh, Dominique Mailloux, Kismet Wells, Ali Coblentz,
Erik (the jerk whom I forgive) Zarjuban, or even ever-absent landlord
Todd Something.
O how everyone turns away from their leisurely, innocent human position—
     Wait, attaining repose of conscience
   So anyway done with due edification, the switching boxcars
clank across the range and a far-off feral dog howls at the waning moon
and from elucidating pasty clouds out ooze the night's inexplicably soft
biblical stars. That is, the third is more perfect in itself than the second,
and the second than the first, and that's that.
   My poet thoughts go through my head: ephemeral actions
heave, slant, arc, break apart into the bright loam of reverential Heaven.
   In all I am tranquil. Contrariwise nearing 30 and contemplating
appetitive powers of the soul, when will I decide to give up online dating
apps?
   Alone and shouldering inert birds of marble at 19:13, I slouch
towards the light. The world's forsaken cry flows through my bare feet
bottoms
(For brevity's sake, we omit it here)

The Coast

Fog engulfs the strand,
its denizens' voices are veiled
in the mist of a briny dream

The monologue of babbling water
swelling from the saline depths
meeting the monolithic shoreline
tunes into the psyche unseen
the brutal tenderness
veiling the color of those
who weave the coast
where the waifs of the tide bore in as
a roaring wall of water,
and small gullies gush,
flattening sands
of time panning out
reflecting a fogged sky
now soon to bear away
the surging hush of surf
possessed by far-off tempests

Overhead I can see the outline of a pale, careless sun,
almost feel its warmth,
the living life and the sea-wind sun-blurred breeze
I can taste, allowing it to taste my face too
raw and stubbly grains
of sand somehow landing
where they should

After a while
I remove the veil or rather
the clouds do
and I begin to see and hear—
a requisite
of the great undulating seas
pulsing the open ocean
roaring a singular, everlasting, mingling
consistent and wet
perfectly powerful
symphony of surf

Crowds of small rippling waters,
more like spots of surreal spotted sea foam,
whine and crawl at my feet as the refluent ocean peels away from the shore
in a slowing, indolent approach
I outrun them.

Locating

To Nehalem's King, Travis Champ

The elements of night that which we share:
the waxing moon, the whispering sea, the turbulent collapsible distance
on this side of black holes
intertwining beyond location.

My prayer is also expanding
back toward the familiar
pendulous pulse of water
in the one breath it takes flesh to collide
in dry sand
and a shell bore witness
beneath the surface.

It has been too long since
our first parting, so many parts of us
having lain separated like this in a sound
relocated
at the edge of night. Together
we have been transmuting æons
in the throes of stars
until dawn.

Distances

Distant and eyeing
the majestic beauty of me not being able
to see things as they are below
but now
I am peering into an abyss—
the flats of cities
filled with the foolish
of mind and I am foolish
and still listening to the earth's wild spectrum of color
until distance diminishes eager desire
enthroned atop a ridge of scree in ageless suspension
where space reigns supreme, I peer
into a deep-delved fissure of the Earth
aglow within sunset clouds, where I am
beset by questions of spiritual synchronicity
within the light beauty ranges
pushing upwards gravely with God's Northwest dew
while lichen, growing on alpine rock,
is redeemed by wilderness
and the earth's reckless prodigals below
scheme in their preservation of self
in boundless determination
and I can see them and the vision
of the seer never ceases on nature's insistence
on the kinship of all living things
within or without
distance in the eye.

Termoli Chant

O reachless seascape spaces listen to me talk on against the limitations of time
as the crest of a wave peals in a crescent moon's cycloramic canticle
of blue sea-wind infatuating the blinking calm of fierce abstract eye
death subtracted by spirit, then measured to by
the confusion of the cathedral's tolling belfry careening and
undone by logic bells swelling with light,
shells crushing the perishing beach dancing into doom
below the sinking tidewaters' patterns scattering
in shadow for miles underlying tumorous waves retreating
before I hesitate, surfacing the fathoms
as surreal spotted sea foam in oxidizing bloom as if,
crestfallen, Her Majesty were singing,
"this is a sea of reality."

The smell, the taste
of the sea, of the worm
is the smell, the taste
of tears manumitting
fresh rain conjuring
sea-levels
one drop
at a time knowing
nothing about rust
or deception.

Autumn's Equinox

To B. Calliope Lynch

Migrating beyond
the passing summer
in suggestions of the rolling land's
cooling wind blowing
that the leaves must go
the mute intentness in a syncopated whorl of death's dropping patter
to cover a brown meadow in autumnal tints
before dusk's long purple fingers unfurling the loam
of the withering wildflower
votive and stuck in an unquestioning manner
right before the goose-eye view
and the slanted sun's radiant eye stuns us
fixed upon the serried blue boughs of skeletal trees
minute quivering innervations of green-warmth
squalling lamentations of the wind, the sighing breath
of a temperamental ventriloquist
now caught in the throes of mercurial changing moods
over unseen roots wresting whims into the world's
turning wood together
beneath a backdrop of changing hues
still and for a passage of time,
never up to you nor I
in the swift senescent winter glare
acquiescing in one reinforced body the lonely ache and presence
cluttering up the life of the season as it never skips its turn
and dies

Dropping leaves are fall's dream
and if you catch my eye, like a withering meadow flower
I might forget while the woods remember
a fire singing through the trees
bargaining with the sun is autumn's dream.

Monologue

The monolithic hum of the hills'
sigh and pulse reverberates
under the dizzying blue heights of space—
a lulling light,
stock still in the mid sky
sends itself back
as the moon rises and arcs
breathing a sigh
of coolness taut by silence,
while the shooting stars
cross the tune of hearts'
steady cadence created
by judgment of our inside

Dawn winds cut
through high peak
shrouded in cloud
through mantles of thick conifer
through the votive labyrinth
of mind stirring a delicate persuasion
glinting everywhere
like when we look at the sun
and close our eyes
all we see inside our eyelids
is the magic of earth

Contemplating the flow of life and change
of all living things reliant
upon cloud, snow, light
under the same sky
in lucid monologues
about new discoveries taking place
inside ourselves
at once holding them close,
in order to give them away.

Theo-logy

Bio Rio, Stockholm
Theo selflessly dances—
a superior creature
in spirited evolution
on the pupal stage
histoblasting his way before the alcoves of moving pictures
as a moving phosphorescent shadow
of lives made real by the sudden twists reeling in His ominous mind
taking aim at the vulnerable and stringing along man's ectoplasmic jelly —
finding the least resistance in empathy, where larvae try not to offend
on the path of metamorphosis

Enlightened Theo —
excuse the excuse
but, because
He's innocent —
merely
making copies of himself
to shine on Heaven, leading us into the unknown
with sympathetic magic
so we can find our way
when the picture stops.

Alis Volat Propriis

To the good pedagogy of Dennis Denisoff

Please imagine larvae
building thick cocoons of comfort
as an embryonic metamorphosis into words,
where there are terminable bits of cold flesh
fecundating, half decaying, half larval
outside the confines of linear time
separating from the host of an unknown
origin
behind a decadent monstrosity of teeth.

A jelly
a tissue
a growing putrescence of artifice
a kernel of sequential eternity
likely to take root and grow any
where there are frequencies,
sliding apertures
of perception's
intended notions
open and close and reflect at once
the susurrus beating of wings
weaving a mass of static shadow
vanishing into nothing as
a repetitive whisper abuzz and lasting for longer than you think,
much like the dry hum
of a moth's wings rubbing together
inaudible.

Lost in movement of thoughts
and full of thoughts
about being tough
taking flight
on a surface of inertia regarding
our civilization
as a miasmic swamp of salient claws scrubbing together
the shapes of which, through reflection, are seen
anew in waiting,
in yearning
for tomorrow before it arrives
under the ominous ticking

of an unseen timepiece
it is an even tenor hum
and like infinite treachery,
it adopts a linear lexicon of ambivalence,
an everlasting hush
(a hush of eternity).

Warped in torpid
personal topics spat
to the tune of our psyche unseen
white lies where there's no line of reason to grasp so,
in defiance of fear
we are left gasping
for familiarity on all sides—
etched in a glowing
tint of finality
(of doom)—
straining in imagination,
after an asceticism seems to me to be
our one everlasting origin.

Flying Stand-by

The day is getting bright
The cabin is stuffy
My dry eyes ache already

I'm awake
I'm sitting with my many types of fake appearances
Now, again, who am I?

I don't want to drink
We're all racing around terminals too fast
Our exhaust hurts the unsubstantial air I embrace

Last night I was ill at ease
And this morning more so
Morose I stood-by for this flight

—It annoys me to speak, and it hurts me not to, or rather it's like, but not like a distant closeness, but I've already written that somewhere else. I mean it's like a dilation of the whole universe —

The jets rumble
Seats struggle
The mirrors tremble puddles

I'm sitting for hours straight
I lost my pillow
My phone got broken last week

I've not done much
Loved too little
And I'm tired.

I Went to D.H. Lawrence's Ranch

With my mother
and I immediately feel guilty
I wish I'd come here alone.

I'm annoyed by all her questions, like who is Mabel—
O Mother,
Mother, who am I?
when I'm trying to have a silent moment alone with Lawrence in the slow
heat of the pure sun-substance seated
on a bench beside where he eternally rests
stationary in concrete, nearby Frieda
consumed by my own nothingness
sets of flies swarm my bare toes—
all about us there is the premonition of movement
(like when we finally decide to leave which I don't want to do anyway
in the rental car down the gravel hill
noticing the silent hush of the moon already out above
us under the brown alpine arid pines dropping their needles in the dirt
of a browner loam)—
the growing undertone of wind moans
and I moan too
under my breath in suppressed annoyance at the constant anguish of
patience
that everything takes
in hopeless want of recovering something of my instinct.

Once Jen came here alone and has now scrammed to parts unknown
with someone else in the same way I walked
through a glimpse of her walking trodding the long furtive line of neutrality
in one motion we departed from each other.
Wow. And once all my other dolls with their D.H. Lawrence problems
were at once mine to share, up and left.
And I now know that I didn't know what my intuition was telling me.
Well,
Tilde I do miss terribly— she quoted you all the time you know.

I'm not much of a son or a lover

San Luis Obispo

Unanswered calls gone unreturned,
what a splendid country full of indecision!

I am a transient circumstance, a man with a finite range of limited understanding

There is a group of us newly acquainted fieldworkers
tipping back s.l.o.(w) cappuccinos called Gibraltars— the sensation which that glassy
material object will give us as we bask together as one gray morning light smudged
on the sidewalk of the same color, agreeing in that kind of hoarse morning tone
they taste like how the Surfliner Caltrain across the street looks
parting the air with the sound of fog through the semi-gloom
haze of summer marine layer lulling us
by the clanking of its sleek radiance that might explode in coming night
calling out dormant Morros, but the coffee still tastes more delicious than the train
looks below the Rock where we came to paddle out in one belly shape
dilating the whole universe of pulsing water carrying the pressure of our own existence

How we paddle and paddle
like motion without thought
thinking the ocean
will never stop
surfers from performing the perennial pop up
looking over our shoulders
at the horizon
forever given over to listening to the sea unseen unfolding beneath the surface of our breath showing us where the night begins, the droning disquisitions of yore such as suggesting an everlasting continuum of everything we know breaking in waves, like the inexactness of quoting a fact: there is one moon, one sun, one Rock, maybe two Rocks— after all, exceptions prove rules— wrested first by the Phoenicians, or the Greeks, then all denominational Iberians, perhaps the Berbers at one point, then the British there in the Strait— an interlude— all things the all-glorious sun operating on the star system witnesses and summer will not outlast these uncertain victories— the swelling epiphany that the Rock will someday be somebody else's regardless of painful opinions swinging through great arcs of approval and disapproval and not once but interminably it is ours in California with the circular breath of the

centuries transpiring across continents and holy languages before an
imperfect presence of friends under an indifferent shifting moon and
well the idea is that the heart endures and always will
while a dull sun pulls
light away under
a mauve dusk

The diurnal diuretic is totally worn off now that we're done surfing and
have switched over to beer and don't discuss its taste because it is obvious
and night
and we are still

The endless duplication of lives becoming quiet objects,
the confluent waves feeding desire in intravenous ways foreshadowing
the knowledge of things foreseen in the bay beyond
the range of loneliness and solitude
calculating what we are capable of knowing in spirit and senses

Proof refutes me, like gravity, like returning the gaze of the ocean, but
not like these new social coefficients of one effulgence who will eventually
undo me standing in a stillness becoming alive— tides and coastlines
will digress and my friends are acting exactly like the ocean in a balancing
act shifting weight from one hip to the other, waiting for something else
to happen— all thoughts and feelings are exchangeable before we
exchanged what were, upon later consideration, lightfelt goodbyes in
those tender moments of quiet ennui I forgot to recognize how keen
everything felt at once under the same old slow-sliding wavelight of
pleasure and foam as the coastal moon swept through us in a parallel
time constraint as might be perceived by the slow blinking eye of
Todd's chameleon I saw locked in its cage of iron-bar-sorrows in another
empty bathroom of mine

Feigning to forget inviolable solitude, I paddle through an old wound
watching the shadows dissolve and reappear crawling to the true bend
of gravity, which is the world's pain I think, searching for symbolism
from that meditative space as the light of a new day waits once I finish
drying my cheeks, spit, get up, and flush.

Quaresima

At about this time I migrated south following the rain's pelt bejeweling a thousand lights of restful-stars winking light in steady cadence with my eyes lining the road in a downpour from the dripping bone of Alaska's rib-coast eventually into Washington, to my old home of ever-shudder U.S.A., where people think I don't understand what it takes to want to be a man—a dream, dreaming, have ever dreamt, and have I ever been dumb struck at everyone withal everywhere with the same hair, same face, same mouth, same thought— moving through the myriad mindless millions I shuffle and when we get deep down to the blood-making-marrow of it, the same shallow lake hollow and coated in ice—e ven when you're home and the only home you've ever had has been in your head, like that which you might've done while dreaming your whereabouts to death— realizing death is always happening in strange transitory vibrations— and never before since Quasimodo roamed the streets of medieval Paris have so many people uttered the phrase, "That poor man"— O please God, my Pa my Jim my Uncle Franky and O my dear dear sweet Joe, don't desert me now ("I don't believe in Buddha, I'm where they cremate people, in a mausoleum!")— eyeing perfect wood stacks of lost purity that make you think of the body of Oregon it's like a miracle, it's the prodigious valley of the Willamette with her wood-piles lumbering into Portland's smoking pulp mill eternity under the tapping needle-sluice rain on a thousand brimming bridges opening and leading to eternal bristling pines rimming the ridges—me shuffling forth the forlorn begrimed street corner of unchangeable Time shuddering with shame and pressing my nose up against the windowpane without lines on my face showing like fear can't in public to peer in at the current gamut of the deleterious faces with obvious distaste sneering back with cool, radiant eyes—O I should have, ah, I shoulda shoulda shoulda *shibuki*— shuddering a patch of fog-breath through the vast face space of emptiness, believing this trending lumberjack-ramen-canoodle-town of Oregon fitting perfectly together with a small obscure maple-leafed-Jap-monk-hands-of-a-komuso-flapjack-flipping-hamlet like a jigsaw puzzle piece, although it isn't quite as simple as all that at all— the way the contours of the wind point all wayward ways toward the jagged loneliness of sunless cliffs of some monolithic Pacific Hibachi coastline, and more so after a long bereft separation from Ass-storia— where now there too sits the requisite honey colored creature with tiny suppurate spots on her face as delicate as the designs on a Geisha's teacup— standard time ticks on her flattering falsehoods of feasting shuddering all great supper charms all about her antidepressant popping, frenzied book reading feminist (granddaughter) of a Swedish sawyer out to dinner with her Pa who now scowls at the jubilance of men when once she would exalt in phrases like, "ladies night all the girls drink for free"—ah, Time—myriad wingless squawking streets as forgotten teacups full of ash float by she sees propped up at the seki with golden trellises of hair fanning over shoulder, a willful volition revealing every greasy stubbly leg hair grown over shy thigh, an extension of another set of dimpled knees swaying in pendulous sea-motion— the sweet love fevers yes and up the middle of her once upturned skirt rests the one and only center of independent ecstasy allying those aforementioned knees now flushed against the windowpane in dampening dusk— it is a wet noiseless hum of Time in a desultory sighing universe without, shuddering under an everlasting tempest teacup & bowl of hot dumpling spicy egg soup— in the rain I break my pace, run out of time, sigh, am lost shuffling & fingering my genitalia through my rain slicker's pocket lining like a Chekhovian character . . . O lost as ever, I accept a lost whereabouts forever.

Westward Reflection

Devoid of caution and full of sanguine expectation
here I was once swept away by a prairie gust, peering thru soft morning light,
where I once heard a creaking stillness of a running creek
as if it were a kaleidoscopic unity
of light and sound
glinting still as one

I recall moment being resolute in the face of danger here—
where my energies of mind were not once challenged
but now are drenched in eye-pride
where a thin stream of tearlets
becomes a sudden warm torrent
and I muse in the reckoning
that my blood's memory
can count catastrophe

So I returned following an abiding hope
in powerless committal
a fool chase as if after a buffalo

Remembering our one stiff skin thick as tree trunks, and
that one voice of yours sounding sweet in the conflagration of night's evening air
sweet and cool upon precious of light holding you
is still one of my many fevered fancies in imagination
"it's still just you and me here"
of yore in a myriad-swarming virgin sound

This sound swore to bear me and my destiny— crouching, panting—
you still cool,
when you in fact cheered at no small rate,
"Come, come, come"
in the dawn's flushing light,
I kissed your ribs
giving way to my heart
nothing I did per se,
atop this once golden ridge, and in that same cool manner of speaking you said,
"nature still qualifies me to become a mother"

It has been a year now since I wanted nothing,
and once everything was taken away
by currents swifter than any horse can run,
my courage leapt at the chase as if blind and corrupt from within
a hopeless task
and so I gave up
who I once was
flaking into dust

Now here where we met on the ridge I crouch
on my haunches alone in a different sort of panting
still in the soft light,
still glinting under the raze
of a setting sun

Talking to a taciturn winter wind
a memory within bellows,
which I'll leave to the natural order of attrition
a corrupt heart committing itself to one singular and perverse intention

And I kneel down before the rock that once cradled you and all you were
"not always, but in all probability still"

I'll be stretched thin
in a stiffness of fierce abstraction— pity

but anyway and forever, I'll be found here
resolved and for all outward appearances
at peace with the four points
of a wind

Please give baby a kiss, no two of them, and take one for yourself.

Tuesday Morning Trying on Death

Lying on the floor miring into a fugue state staring limply at the ceiling

In the peripheral distances, he sees the clock,
measuring its ticking motion not wanting to admit that time's up

He pulls the crimson
carpet over his face
away from his mouth
so *he* can breathe
to curse himself
his body tremulous
of what is at once an opaque pain and futility,
of what is both justice's fullness and life's wane
a veritable echo in his mind
toward some unknown pinnacle
a lost hum of Time

I grope for sleep by closing my eyes
seeing, in slumbering lure,
a cadaverous figure waiting
in the center of a cobweb shawl
remembering my dream unwreathed among perennial hordes of harrowed lords
consummating hate and misery in shrouded shadow
with impenetrable veneration in their eyes, canticles & harmonies in immobile lips
an unseen tremor those who dream know
Time and space are one

With a tumult in my nuanced chambered chest
I roll on the floor
bleeding for three
silent, sinister, and purposeful
as a virulent convergence.

Broad Creek Run

You have put your hands through my hair reddening my face in the cold, and the heat in my ears you too have whispered sophisms of madness bellowing me across the continent to nowhere in my restless dragging where your face, flushed like the dawn on the riverbank, is weeping a stand of furrowing trees, barking brown mosses adorned all around your broken stillness above the screaming air traversing jetliners.

The mysticism of stony cliffs. Nothing stirs below. The brown river is smooth on my eye, is slick as glass. The dead moss lies interred under colorless leaves. The large groaning stones stay fixed to give the cliff its face looks back at my shadow out of eternity in my arm leaning over a green plastic picnic bench engraved with strange etchings.

The glazed sun pulls itself over derisive rocks rising above great trees full of mystery and antiquity. The river froths over a row of protruding rocks therein. Does their purpose stop or begin?

The impossible totality dissolved into something complete and great, something isolated, something detached. I cannot see if some life rhythm has been disturbed. On the bank I search desperately (I need to start stop taking B's prescriptions).

Intrusive thoughts, like how the sight of an old lover's eye in the morning opened wide contents me. O algebraic lyricism of life. I am getting hung up on make-believing this is real so I might see it all the time. Unlike the slow moving Potomac, I am sighing less than usual, and the quick change is so obvious that it's beyond reason.

Somehow still the earth will recoil and repel what I notice without a flicker of the eye is nothing but desecration.

Currently

To @sugartits

Wending our way upon the weather-beaten trail of abandoned warping wood train track
above West Boylston's reservoir where
wings unwind in silence,
tongues of fern hang out,
steady ticks come in from the thickets of lichen, and one by one
hidden birds in late afternoon sunlight are defined
as objects, and our footsteps begin
crossing and re-crossing
my scabbed toes curling in Birkenstocks, yours doing the same in Blundstones
through luminous humidity seeking to intertwine the other stammering
to a menagerie of vines consuming didactic limbs to make straight our sexual ways
and are each ignored inexorably as sweet rivulets of sweat, in a beading unified clip clap
motion swing from the myth of ascending, we, as one, are currently joined and slipping
between the trees of light upon a tryst of fleeting lust that never falters into the pleasant plane
of our two green natures amid the scorching New England overgrowth.

A soft plenitude. What we do now will probably hurt somebody else.

The venery of
lifting up
your bulging
midriff I
wrap an arm around
from behind
we grip down and be-
gin to awaken every
thing so tense and so
wet stretching one skin
behind your breathing breasts
lying in a land of dreams
I stoop into with avid hands
groping forth every
where our liquid cross-eyed
stare penetrates

what is wet
we are sweating
"dirty rail trail sex"
 you said so—

Things working together as one
light separates our skin in
the wetness of all good things

Afterwards in the parking lot I see you for a moment, the silver gleam
of your eyes
bending a shaft of air and light streaming
through your car's cracked window
you've just come in from the lyrical blooming spring,
your head bent demurely to the sun, lazy and
smiling, ambivalent, being.
A nerve twists.
I feel like I've been lingering too long and unwanted
like a wart or like a sunset in Madrid because it is silent
and what difference does it really make that I'm standing here?
The stark dignity of exit I know perfectly well, well as any dude can
that you're waiting for me to walk away so you can
get on with your responsibilities
and still we'll go onto even hotter, greater ambivalence
later, and will be cool
at our next rail trail crossing
paths will not be suntans and scabs,
the distance of our not-so-unique cross-eyed stare in the late afternoon
is not like butterfly bodies
light yearly migrations
apace from each other
nothing pushes us away
even now currently bending
my gaze to the sun above the reservoir I peripherally see yet another
lover's complacent, silver eye-look in you becoming green
as I reach a meek hand in to wipe the rail trail sweat
from your face.

Sonnet 70, Massachusetts

To Nicholas Palumbo

I wake up tired from all the gathering madness. My back is bellowing from traveling through too many different beds. I am a little hung-over. Piper gone to Indiana, Murray to work— I only heard a few alarms. It's an early June morning. It's eleven. Because it's still spring I put on last summer's torn shorts and a white stained wife beater. I walk through the muggy street to the rail trail beginning to sun to sit by the curving river reminding me of the crooked parenthesis drawn in Anvina's Cyrillic hand for an art project I saw in Bennington. It is actually a tributary of the reservoir. In a lost impulse, I contemplate the froth and things, but they remind me of nothing, so I come home and write about those things and boil water. I'm alone. I feel like I've been lingering too long. I've read somewhere that good intentions are an act of aggression, so I wash yesterday's dishes to contribute something to the household. Water's boiled and I pour green tea of my tears. I'm buzzed. I read June poem from Bradley on my phone about 2020 and egg yolks. I've never written a sonnet, so I stop in the middle of his to make breakfast at five past one, read my poems "That Mattered in the Moment" skipping the ones imitating Wolfe. I return to Bradley's— I hate phones— after flipping through the cookbooks on the shelf —
Babe Crocker, *Cocktails*, 3 of them by Jamie Oliver, *Test Kitchen*.
I still can't cook.
I wonder if Claudia, or Nadine, or Louise ever think about me
I wonder if Rasmus Meilvang still dislikes me, why Mark Calvarese won't reply, if Michael Albanese and Falcone forgive me, if Hiram Reynolds trusts me,
I wonder if people talk about me, I wonder if I'm cold to my parents
I wonder if I'm fooling myself about contributing anything here
I wonder what there is to eat in the house apart from eggs and grapefruits
I wonder if Murray will bring home beer.

Renga

Nonselective fog
sweeps the midday leaves with rain
in the early fall
bare toes wince through frosting grass
picking summer's last clover.

Earth holds together
shades: orange, red, yellow, brown
changing the seasons
through benevolent discourse
blinking emotion away.

Now the snow lies heaped
on the stones a harvest moon
shines, though there's no work
the seasonal flower blooms
squalls of frost and snow tonight.

Morning dew, spring sun
even the goose knows
what season it is.

Skaneateles Post Office

The mail lady at the post office is a positive informant.
Her fluorescent black hair is upheld
by its own accord, and she talks in kind, definitive phrases

At once I started comparing her in my mind
the differences and similarities
to my Aunt, who shares her name and who used to remind me
in my youth to put the right postage on the packages she knew I'd send along
because she worked for the Post Office
and my childhood piano teacher named Regina
"Middle C is a landmark, like the cemetery or the post office in the village"
and this mail lady Amy has their likeness

I don't know why the system won't let me send the package, she says
Spain. Restrictions. Independence Day weekend.
You might try another post office if it's convenient for you to see if
they can tell
— dental floss, a letter—
It'll cost at least 40 dollars to send these Priority. Do you care how fast
they arrive there?

She peels off the green marigold stamp
with neat, dexterous fingers handing it to me
You should glue this onto a padded envelope instead of a Priority box.
I'm sorry we couldn't get this to send
she says with her cracked toothy smile as I push open the door,
Check back in a couple days. It'll save you a lot of money if you don't
send it as Priority.

Outside
her kindness has set the birds
in the splintered spectacle of the trees as bars of a song to flight
above the primal fluorescent loam of tulips
the height of summer has come
to Skaneateles.

END

The dim twilight
the punctual respiration of the Earth
the sky faintly pearled in the surprisingly grapefruity bloom
of dawn the syncopation of which
is blue and here you are,
carrying your baggage and
visiting my sleep
like a surprised pilgrim in a strange country.

The chromaticism of your footsteps
curdles, drifting to the top
of the bluish milk of bedroom doors.

How can I tell you that rain is a clock on the window?

You wonder what land this is, what love is
like this seems like Spain,
and really I am like Sweden.

The trembling blue pines out the window
shake me into dreaming the true
colors of autumn
all about your pursed lips, as if my furrowing forehead
were sibilate and ready for kissing
as my green eyes spring to bloom
the ecstasy of always bursting forth.

You take off the dress
I gave you and I see
you taking the glass bottle of perfume
from your suitcase I once
gave you, setting it aside
and I wonder where the green saint medallion on a silver chain
you gave me is on the milk crate bedside table
and I should give you more.

What ever happened to those mornings when we solved everything?

Sitting on the edge
of the bed I hold your hand.

I wake up, and this vision
is not only packed but gone
and a feeling like being choked enters my throat,
and it is raining, softly raining.

Nicholas Skaldetvind spent his boyhood around the Finger Lakes of New York. He is a graduate of Stockholm University's English Department, where he wrote his Master's thesis on the spontaneous poetics of Jack Kerouac's letters. Above all else, Nicholas is a freelance country gentleman.

"Nicholas Skaldetvind writes in a lava flow of haunting images. By incorporating a quiet empathy to underlie his musings, he pays elegant homage to the Beats with a searching, self-deprecating honesty that makes me want more. Skaldetvind's voice is transparent, kind, and unpredictable: a voice for our time."

~Jim Ellis, Auburn Poetry Circle

"Nicholas Skaldetvind weaves through his verse a voice that is immediately and delightfully contemporary at the same time threads allusions to the dead poets he admires, tucked into his poems as in an urban bird's nest. Longing for Romantic heights, his speaker's voice is both richly mellifluous and mundanely self-deprecating— less D.H. Lawrence and more Prufrock— balancing between poignancy and humor. Some images are fresh, liquid lucidity, while at other times Skaldetvind seems to recognize that the modern poet is inevitably a tourist among the great artifacts of the language. This is a vital and worthy volume."

~Paul Schreiber, Poetry Editor, *Two Thirds North*

www.ingramcontent.com/pod-product-compliance
Lightning Source LLC
Chambersburg PA
CBHW050335120526
44592CB00014B/2192